Shamanism for Beginners

Otherworld Journey and Ancestor Worship, Sweat Lodge and Firewalk

Contact: www.HarryEilenstein.de
Harry.Eilenstein@web.de
Harry Eilenstein at youtube

Production and publishing house: BoD - Books on Demand, Norderstedt

ISBN: 9783753454146

Shaman, Siberia, 1692

for Jörg Wichmann †,
my best friend for decades

Table of Contents

I What is a Shaman?

The shaman is the religio-spiritual-magical specialist of the Old Stone Age and consequently also of today's primitive peoples, who still live largely like our ancestors in the Old Stone Age.

The shamans have a central task-area: the establishment of the contact to the ancestors in the beyond.

A shaman become a shaman by experiencing a near-death, e.g. almost being eaten by a hungry bear. During such an experience the soul ("astral body") leaves the physical body and floats above it, i.e. one sees oneself lying underneath. Thus one experiences very clearly that one is more than only one's own physical body. Such an experience one can have quite consciously or also without consciousness – in the second case it is a simple fainting. But even in the case of fainting, one often still has a diffuse memory of having watched oneself faint like an outsider.

If a person who has experienced such a near-death has been curious enough to explore how one can consciously and willingly leave one's own physical body, he had acquired the ability to go into the "soul-state". Since the ancestors also no longer have a body and are only a soul, these people, who were able to leave their bodies willingly, had the possibility to consciously and intentionally make contact with other souls as well – and consequently to establish contact between the living and their ancestors.

Such a person had then become a shaman. He was from then on responsible for the care of other people who had experienced a near-death, for the otherworld journey to the ancestors and for leading the sweat lodge, in which the ancestors were also summoned.

Since at that time one received all advice and help from one's parents (there were no schools and no social security at that time), one turned to one's parents for advice and help even after the death of them. Thus, the idea arose that all help comes from the other world – including magical help. Therefore, the shaman as the one "who speaks with the ancestors" was also responsible for every form of magic.

II   Shamans and Shamanesses

It is difficult to assess whether there were originally only male shamans, only female shamans, or both. First of all, both man and woman can experience a near-death and consequently can become a shaman or a shamaness.

On the pictures of the Paleolithic, however, only male animal dancers are to be seen and also from the Neolithic there are only male representations which can be understood as shamans. Likewise, in the epoch of kingship only priests with shaman function are found, but no priestesses with shaman function. The exception to this are the priestesses on Crete, who hold two snakes in their hands – they could possibly be shaman priestesses.

In the nature religions the shamanesses are mostly responsible for healing with the help of herbs and for births. Only in some areas of northeast Africa and in some cults such as Voodoo and Candomblé, which also originated in Africa, are there predominantly female shamans and less frequently male shamans.

In some cultures the female shamans interrupt their activity for some years after the birth of a child as well as during menstruation – which leads to the fact that the most important female shamans are mainly older women.

Possibly, this finding can be explained by the fact that in the hunter culture of the Paleolithic, it was mainly the men who had near-death experiences while hunting and could therefore become shamans. Possibly there have always been isolated female shamans, but so rarely that they do not appear in the tradition. However, it is not even completely sure that some women were not at least sometimes part of the hunting groups too …

However, one must also consider that there are only very few pictures of shamans from the Paleolithic as well as from the Neolithic, what makes sure conclusions very difficult. Possibly there were also female shamans in the Paleolithic, but only animal dancers and no female animal dancers – perhaps because animals were also associated with hunting.

In any case, it can be stated that today both men and women can have a near-death experience and have the ability to repeat this experience at will and to develop it in such a way that they can become shamans or shamanesses.

III Astral Projection and Kundalini

One becomes a shaman primarily by experiencing a near-death ("astral projection") and then learning to repeat this experience willingly.

There are three different methods to leave one's own body consciously, willingly, and temporarily – like a shaman.

1. Meditation: Meditation is probably the oldest of the three methods. It quite simply is an imitation of the state of death or fainting. The way to the otherworld and the way to one's own soul is the same way – that is why e.g. the Tibetan Book of the Dead is at the same time a description of what happens after death and a meditation instruction.

By this imitation of death one comes into the inner silence and finds the contact to the own soul. During near-death the soul leaves the body ("astral projection") and the body becomes motionless – during meditation the body becomes motionless and the soul may leave the body. By the representation of the characteristics of the near-death the state of near-death is evoked … One can understand some meditations therefore also as a willfully brought about swoon.

The forms of meditation that can lead to the experience of astral travel are the various relaxation exercises, self-hypnosis, autogenic training and the like. These forms of meditation lead to a gradual shift of consciousness from the physical body to the life force body ("astral body"): Through relaxation, the perception of the physical body fades away to an increasing degree – at the same time, the life force body moves into perception in the form of heaviness, warmth and an inner vibration of 6Hz, until it finally detaches from the physical body and can then move freely in space independently of it.

As a side effect, these exercises can also evoke the inner silence, which in turn can lead to a direct perception of one's own soul. This "filled silence" is the state of soul-consciousness and also the state of deep sleep.

2. Ecstasy: Ecstasy is a method to achieve one-pointedness. When one is unreservedly, unrestrainedly one-pointed, what one is so resolutely one-pointed toward happens – including the otherworld journey.

To achieve this state, shamans use mostly the beating of a steady beat on a drum. The steady sound helps to align one's consciousness. All of today's trance dances also have a loud, steady rhythm as a basic element – the movements of the body and the alignment of the consciousness resonate to this beat.

The drum used is a frame drum (tambourine) – this is the simplest drum, which was created by stretching a skin on a circularly bent branch in order to tan and work it.

Otherworldly scenes are often painted on this drum – especially the world tree as the path between this world and the otherworld.

3. Drugs: The third and probably most recent method is to use drugs that induce a death-like state. If one errs with the dosage of the poisonous plants used for this purpose, there is a danger of actually dying. This very dangerous method is therefore a near-death brought about by poison.

Closely related to astral projection is a second phenomenon: Kundalini. This phenomenon consists essentially of the experience of intense heat rising in one's own body. If the shamans have practiced astral projection, they will almost inevitably have discovered Kundalini as well.

The reason that these two phenomena are closely connected is that in order to attain both experiences, one spends most of the time becoming conscious of one's life force body (astral body, soul). This awareness begins with relaxing, then feeling heavy, then feeling warm, and finally feeling one's body begin to vibrate at about 6Hz. These are also the same phenomena that are used to induce hypnosis: "You are relaxed, you feel your body become heavy, you feel your body become warm ..." (The image of vibration is not used in hypnosis.)

In astral projection, the next step is that the vibrating expands to a swaying and finally to a detachment of the astral body from the physical body: The internal movement becomes an external movement.

In the awakening of the Kundalini fire, on the other hand, the next step is to let the vibrating become an inner movement, a convection current inside the body, which roughly corresponds to the circulation of blood in the physical body: an inner movement. This heat rises inside the body like a jet of water out of a pond, unfolds above the head like a fountain, and then flows down around the outside of the body like a drops and gathers again at the bottom of the body.

Through Kundalini, one also becomes aware of the "organs" in the life force body: the chakras.

The life force, the Kundalini and the chakras are the source of magic, that is, of the imprinting of matter by consciousness: telepathy and telekinesis in their many manifestations. Therefore the shamans will have become quite soon also the specialists of magic.

Probably at least telepathy will have been known before the emergence of shamanism: Even today, almost every human being senses when he is stared at from behind

– this has been a telepathic ability necessary for survival at that time, when a hungry tiger snuck up from behind …

IV   The Ancestors

Only 500 years ago, even in Europe, parents were the only support in the world for most people – and they were also the people from whom they "learned life". Without social security, schools, hospitals, police, etc., people depended on their parents in many situations – they were the authority par excellence.

It is therefore not surprising that people have wished to continue to receive advice and support from their parents even after their death. From this arose what in the history of religion is somewhat misleadingly called "ancestor worship".

IV 1.   Paleolithic Age

How the contact to the ancestors may have looked like in the Paleolithic Age is largely unknown. The oldest proven burials are 280,000 years old – they still come from Homo erectus, the ancestors of Homo sapiens.

From the Neanderthal man a skull is known, which was put in a cave on a kind of pedestal, which makes it look like a cult object. The Homo erectus has had 400.000 years ago at a living place in Bilzingsleben in Thuringia several huts, a slaughter place, a garbage place etc., but also a central place, that has been paved with stones, on which stood an altar stone, on which lay a bull skull and fragments of skulls of humans.

So it could well be that already in the Paleolithic Age, for more than 400,000 years, people have used the skulls of their ancestors to continue contact with these ancestors after their death.

Probably also already at that time the sticks standing in a circle and joined together, from which one built a sweat lodge, represented the ancestors, who gave support to their descendants, who sat in the sweat lodge with these vertical sticks stuck in the earth behind them.

The shamans have most likely been responsible for establishing contact with these ancestors. It can be assumed, however, that this contact was in principle open to everyone, but that the shamans were more practiced at it than most other people.

A special form of contact to the ancestors is the once very widespead custom of cannibalism, i.e. the ritual eating of the body of the deceased by his decendents. It is quite probable, that the shamans have also been the leaders of the rites of cannibalism. By these rites the life force and the skills of the dead ancestor were meant to be transferred to his decendents.

IV 2. Neolithic Age

In the Neolithic period, the custom of storing the skulls of the deceased in niches in the walls of dwellings was widespread. They were sometimes covered with clay, which was molded into the most realistic image of the dead.

The sticks of the sweat lodge became the pillars in the early temples of man, which were built half of stone and half of branches and skins 12,000 years ago (Göbekli Tepe, Nevali Cori and others). These pillars stood in the stone piled foundation wall of these sweat lodge temples – so like the sticks in the sweat lodge in a circle. These pillars are clearly recognizable as stylized people because of their arms, indicated eyes, clothes and the like: the ancestors.

When more people lived together and larger temples were needed, the wall of the sweat lodge temples were left out and limited to the circle of ancestor pillars, which were then also replaced by simple rocks. This is how the stone circles of the menhir culture evolved.

Very likely, "stone circles" that consisted only of wooden posts and not of stones were also quite widespread, since wood has almost always been the precursor of stone. The best known "wooden circle" is probably Woodhenge near Stonehenge in southern England.

It can be assumed that in addition to the half-stone sweat lodge temples, the simple sweat lodges from the Paleolithic period still existed at that time. The forerunners of the ancestor pillars in the Neolithic sweat lodge temples will have been not only the sweat lodge poles, but also the wooden totem poles, which are found all over the world except in Africa and which everywhere represent the ancestors themselves or the gateway to them. They range from simple ancestor staffs to complex totem poles. In Göbekli Tepe such totem poles are also to be found instead of the more simple manufactured stone pillars in the walls of the temples.

The conversation with the dead will have been conducted by the shamans while sitting either in front of the skull of the person or on his grave. A brushwood mound (a simplified sweatlodge) was erected on the graves at that time – the pregnant belly of the earth-goddess who would give birth to the dead again in the afterlife. These burial brushwood mounds later became the tumuli.

From the sitting on the brushwood mound or the grave later the "seer seat" has been derived. It is found among the Germanic tribes as the wooden pedestal of the seers and sorcerers, among the Celts as the seat of the druids woven from rowan branches, among the Scythians as the brushwood mound of Papaios, the father of the gods, among the Indians as the pedestal, on which the gods and the yogis sit, with the Egyptians as the flat table on which the shaman-priest called "Sem" ("helper") sits at the burial, as the flat pedestal of the shamans in the Harappa culture on the Indus, etc.

From the image of the water underworld has been derived the motif of the soul or sun returning to this world as a lotus rising from a lake, known from Egypt, India and Central America (Mayas).

IV 3. Age of Kingship

In the epoch of kingship, the sweat lodge staffs, the ancestor staffs, the pillars in the sweat lodge temples and the menhirs of the stone circles eventually became the pillars in the temples and the statues of the gods and the ancestors in these temples as well as the scepters of the gods, godesses, priests and kings.

However, the skull cult of the Old and New Stone Age has been able to persist for a long time. In particular, the custom of drinking from the skulls of the deceased in order to obtain the abilities and blessings of those dead has been very persistent. It is still found today in Tibetan Buddhism and also in Christianity it was common until the Middle Ages to make a pilgrimage to the skull relic of a saint in order to be able to drink from his skull and in this way receive his blessing. Since each saint was responsible for clearly defined helps, healings, blessings etc., one knew at that time exactly from which saint's skull one had to drink with the problem one had.

Also the asking of the ancestors for advice and help at the graves was so widespread at that time that it threatened to push the actual Christian religion into the background – this is the reason why the church condemned these conversations with the dead so vehemently that these conversations in the form of the nightly evocation of the dead at the graves or at the crossroads have become one of the creepiest things known today.

The shamans became the priests in this epoch. The shamans continued to exist only in a special function as otherworldly travelers, funeral priests, coronation priests, seers, and the like – they continued to be responsible for the journey to the other-world. However, this "priest for special tasks" receded more and more into the background over time and finally disappeared altogether.

The priest have been in contrast to the shamans "religious clerks", who had no special abilities but who fulfilled their religious duties.

IV 4. Age of Materialism

In materialism, ancestor worship faded almost completely – the dead were dead and gone and the soul was nothing but a figment of superstitious people's imagination. From this point of view religions were at best pre-logical humanitarian institutions and at worst "opium for the people".

Only in Spiritism this contact to the dead has continued – the Spiritists were in this epoch the last shamans who still existed.

Of course, one could also regard the scientific researchers as descendants of the shamans, since both explore the unknown – but this agreement concerns only the thirst for knowledge, but not the field of activity itself.

IV 5. Age of Globalization

In the meantime, the ancestor cult has found its way back into today's world view under a new name, but with the old functions: the systemic family constellations. This method originates from the South African shamans and has been processed and reformulated by Bert Hellinger in such a way that it appears quite unmagical, unspiritual and unreligious and sounds like a psychological therapy – of course it is also psychologically extremely effective.

In general, the psychologically oriented therapists have taken over many of the tasks of the shamans. The therapists who also use dream journeys and family constellations and possibly have a spiritual background come closest to the earlier shamans in today's Western culture. There are also more and more people who combine the knowledge, methods and traditions of all previous eras and in this way create a new form of "spiritual-magical helper".

They connect among other things the following things with each other:

- (Paleolithic Age): otherworld journeys, sweat lodges, family constellations, presence in the here and now, associative worldview

- (Neolithic Age): myths, rituals, archetypes, collective subconscious, dream journeys, firewalks, analogical worldview (mythology)

- (Age of Kingship): priests, religion, monotheism, the One God, initiation rituals, mysteries, philosophical worldview

- (Age of Materialism): scientific research, psychology, parapsychology, magical research, scientific worldview

- (Age of Globalization): comprehensive systems, ecology, synthesis of different worldviews, social aspects, peace initiatives, global worldview

V   The Mother Goddess

The mother is the central motif in the Paleolithic worldview, as is shown by the many statuettes and engravings of women that have been preserved.

V 1.   The Mother

The female statuettes and the female rock engravings from the Paleolithic period have several characteristics, which, however, do not all occur at the same time in every statuette:

- stooped posture => probably sexual union
- woman/cow mixed form => fertility
- a very corpulent body => enough food, pregnant
- cow horn in the hand => vagina, horn of plenty, fullness
- twofold representation => mother in this world and in the otherworld
- left arm raised, right arm lowered => this world and the otherworld

According to these representations, there were at least three aspects in the conceptions of the mother goddess at that time. These three aspects existed on the one hand in this world and on the other hand also in the hereafter.

The Mother-Goddess in the Old Stone Age		
Aspect	*Area*	
	World	*Otherworld*
Procreation	woman, beloved procreation in this world	re-procreation-beloved re-procreation in the otherworld
Birth	mother Birth of the living	otherworld-mother Rebirth of the dead as soul
Breastfeeding	breastfeeding mother the one who gives nourishment	re-breastfeeding mother origin of the ritual potion symbolism

The shaman will probably also have had the task to establish contact to the mother goddess, if a particularly intensive contact was needed due to the situation. It is unlikely that the contact to the archetypes of the mother was possible only through the help of the shaman – after all, every person carries this image in himself.

Probably the image of the mother was closely connected with the image of the group, i.e. the family or clan.

It can also be assumed that the image of the mother was connected with the summer feast of procreation – after all, this feast is about procreation and birth, which are firmly connected with the mother.

This midsummer procreation festival was necessary at that time, so that the children are born at the beginning of spring and then in the next winter are already somewhat stronger and could survive the winter, which was quite cold at that time in the Ice Age. The same function has in the cold countries the rutting season with the larger animals, which get young only once in the year. Remnants of this festival can be found in very many peoples in Europe, Asia and America, all descended from these Ice Age hunters in Eurasia.

(This necessity had the effect, that most of the humans of the Stone Age have had their sun in the astrologcal sign of Aries – the springtime sign. Thus the people of the Stone Age must have been mostly rash, impulsive, and bold, and must have preferred to life in the Here and Now.)

The aspects of the Mother Goddess are the procreation feast in this world and the re-procreation in the next, the birth in this world and the rebirth in the next, as well as the nourishing (breastfeeding) and the ritual potion (re-nourishing).

V 2. The sweat lodge

The first known hut was built 1.9 million years ago – a stone foundation wall of it has been preserved. Probably there were huts long before that, which consisted only of branches, leaves and possibly skins – of course no remains of them have been preserved. There are such constructions with many mammals and birds: the dens of the wolves, foxes, bears, badgers, otters, rabbits etc., the nests of the birds and some monkey kinds, the dray of the squirrels, the castles and dams of the beavers, and the like. These protective constructions of the early humans could go back thus quite far to their ape ancestors.

It can be assumed that these shelters were associated with the mother's womb – these two were the only "interior spaces" that existed at that time ...

At the beginning of the ice age 600.000 years ago a heating of the huts became necessary. For this purpose, stones were made to glow in a fire in front of the hut and then carried to the center of the hut with the shoulder blade of a deer or a similar bone. If a half-frozen hunter came home, one poured possibly also still some water over the glowing stones in the hut, in order to strengthen the heat in the hut. Today, only the sauna remains of this heating technique …

Even soups could be cooked in this way: One put small, hot stones in a skin bag filled with water, pieces of meat and herbs.

The hut and also the sweat lodge gave protection. Since one received protection on the one hand generally from the parents and from the mother goddess, thus from the clan mother, and on the other hand the hut and the sweat lodge were already associated with the mother's belly, it was obvious to extend this picture and to associate the sticks, from which the hut was reached, with the ancestors.

If one sat in the sweat lodge, one wished oneself sometimes apart from protection and warmth surely also other things like many children or success with the hunt. Since animals were used as "image-adjectives" at that time, some animals will have been gradually associated with the sweat lodge: the soul bird, the strong large predator, the fertile herd animal and the serpent of the underworld anfd of the Kundalini – these are still today the four animals that are invoked in the sweat lodges.

As a specialist in establishing the connection with the ancestors and the mother-goddess, the shaman will have led the meetings in the lodge that explicitly served the contact with the ancestors and the mother-goddess – this is how the sweat lodge ceremony gradually came into being. An essential part of these ceremonies will have been the contact with the ancestors, which is found today especially in the family constellations.

The sweat lodge will also have been associated with the caves painted by the people since 50,000 years – they too are a "sacred interior".

At the beginning of the Neolithic period, sweat lodges became larger and more detailed – they became the first temples. These sweat lodge temples, located at Göbekli Tepe in northern Mesopotamia, consisted of several elements:

- an outer stone ring with a domed roof made of branches and skins – this represented the belly of the mother goddess

- an inner stone ring with a domed roof of branches and skins – this represented the child in the mother's belly

- a connecting wall between the two stone circles – this represented the umbilical cord

- a passage leading to the outer ring – this represented the vagina of the mother goddess

- a stone slab with a hole in front of the entrance, on which sat the two panthers of the goddess, that were carved of stone – these represented the outer end of the vagina of the goddess and the strenght of the godess

- mostly eight pillars in the inner wall, which are strongly abstracted people – they represented the ancestors (the "8" has been the symbol of completeness and of perfection)

- two big pillars in the center of the temple – they represent "body and soul".

Later in the Neolithic period, these temples and the caves with the cave paintings gave rise to the cave temples, which consisted of a passage and a chamber at their end. From this then developed the tumuli – and also the pyramids with the passage leading to them. Also many temples have this ground plan. By leaving out the wall and reducing it to the ancestral pillars, the stone circles were created, which are often connected with a stone avenue that corresponds to the passage to the sweat lodge temple. Also the two large pillars are found in the centre of the stone circles.

The shamans have also been the „priests of the stone-circles".

Overview of the sweat lodge development						
Elements	*Forms*					
	Sweat lodge	*Sweat lodge temple*	*Stone circle*	*Barrow*	*Pyramid*	*Temple*
Inner circle (child)	people	inner dome	inner stone circle	burial chamber slabs	pyramid	temple
Outer circle (mother)	dome	outer dome	outer stone circle	stone circle around tumulus	wall around pyramid	wall around temple
Umbilical cord wall	-	umbilical cord wall	-	-	-	-
Aisle	possibly an aisle (like an Iglu)	aisle	stone alley to the stone circle	corridor to the burial chamber	corridor from temple to pyramid	aisle to the center
Ancestors in circle	wands	ancestor pillars	menhirs	tomb chamber stone slabs	statues	statues
Body and soul	pole with bird on top; totem-pole	two central pillars	two central menhirs	sarcophagus	sarcophagus	central-symbol
Entrance plate with hole	-	entrance plate with hole	-	closed entrance plate	closed entrance	temple gate
Panther at the entrance	-	two panther statuettes	two large menhirs at the begin-ning of the avenue	-	two pylons (towers)	two turrets or pillars

V 3. the umbilical cord

The umbilical cord will have been a symbol for a very long time – it represents the connection between mother and child. Even today's word "religion" alludes to this connection, as it means "reconnection", also in the sense of "support".

The earliest possible representations of such a connection are the female statuettes and female engravings from the late Paleolithic and early Neolithic periods, which show her left arm raised and her right arm lowered – this could represent the Mother Goddess as the connection between the two worlds. The popular motif of the double woman shows that the Mother Goddess has not only been the connection of the two worlds, but that she herself has been seen as these two worlds. This motif of the primeval goddess being the two worlds has been preserved in some earth goddesses, in the Sumerian primeval goddess Tiamat, in the South American female primeval serpent, and the like. This motiv can still be seen as the posture of the magician in the Tarot-card "Magician".

A second motif, which may also have been an umbilical symbol, is the staff on which a bird sits. This motif has been depicted in cave paintings and is found in all cultures on earth. It therefore seems to originate at least from the early Homo sapiens – but perhaps it is much older and was already used by Homo erectus. It represented the soul bird – the staff either indicated flying or the connection to the mother goddess, whereby the former is initially more simple and therefore more probable.

The first completely safe representation of the umbilical cord is found in the temples of Göbekli Tepe, where it connects in the form of a short wall the outer mother stone circle with the inner child stone circle, in which also the people sit during the ritual.

The bird pole has evolved into the totem pole, which at first was nothing more than a large bird pole: a man with his soul-bird on his head. However, by the beginning of the Neolithic period, these simple "bird poles" had already become complex totem poles with panthers, ancestors, skulls, snakes (Kundalini), the double goddess, etc. Probably these totem poles were the first representations of complex ideological contexts besides the pictures of the cave paintings.

From the totem poles, which were in the Paleolithic originally carved out of tree trunks before they were also made out of stone in the early Neolithic period, the world tree evolved as the umbilical cord between heaven and earth, between this world and the next.

Through the association of the world tree umbilical cord with the hill grave and the mountain as the belly of the pregnant earth goddess, the umbilical cord symbolism has also been transferred to the sacred mountain, which then became the mountain of the gods.

21

This umbilical cord was the "working path" of the shamans – along it they traveled to the otherworld to the mother goddess and to the ancestors. It is therefore not surprising that the world tree in the form of a staff has become the symbol of the shamans. Later it became the seer's staff and the scepter of kings and finally the magic wand.

So in the Neolithic period the shaman was also a "staff-bearer".

The umbilical cord			
Symbol etc.	*Elements*		
	World	*Connection*	*Otherworld*
Double goddess	upper half	goddess	lower half
Twofold goddess	left arm up	goddess	right arm down
Bird stick	man (stick)	bird on top	soul bird
Totem pole	man (pole)	bird on top	bird
Sacred pipe	man (smoking)	tube of the pipe	pipe bowl
Statue	man	bird on head or shoulders	bird
Scepter	man	scepter	gods
Wand	man	wand	gods
Myths	earth	world tree	sky
Myths	earth	mountain of the gods	sky
Sweat lodge	people	invocation	ancestors
Sweat lodge temple	inner stone ring	umbilical cord wall	outer stone ring
Pyramid	valley temple	corridor	pyramid
Stone circle	exterior	stone avenue	stone circle
Barrow	corridor	corridor	burial chamber
Temple	exterior	corridor	central room
"Religion"	man	religion	gods

VI   The animal symbolism

In the Paleolithic period, almost only animals were moulded, carved, engraved, and painted – the exception being the mother statuettes and the depictions of animal dancers.

Since the frequency of the animals depicted differs greatly both from the frequency of animals in the habitat of the Stone Age hunters at that time and from the frequency of animals in their diet (recognizable from the bone remains), these animal portrayels cannot be a simple representation of their environment or their diet. These animals must therefore have a symbolic meaning – they were, so to speak, "image-adjectives" according to the character of the specific animal.

One can assume that these symbolic animals will have played an essential role in the world view of the shamans of that time.

VI 1.   The soul bird

The soul bird is one of the oldest symbols. It originated from the fact that the life force body hovers above the physical body during astral projection (near-death experience). The terms "soul", "astral body" and "life force body" all refer to the same thing in this context.

The earliest depiction of a soul bird is from the late Paleolithic period and is a bird staff next to a (nearly?) dead hunter.

In Native American sweat lodges, the soul bird appears as the eagle in the east, symbolizing expansiveness, overview, and forethought.

Since one can become a shaman by having a near-death experience, that is, by experiencing oneself as a soul bird, the soul bird is closely connected to shamanism. The ancestors also become soul birds at their death, often sitting on the world tree, where they are visited by the shaman on his otherworld journeys and asked for advice and help for their descendants.

VI 2.   The great predator

The large carnivore symbolizes strength and, above all, success in the hunt. Since Paleolithic hunters also desired this power and hunting success, they identified themselves with the large predator. This symbolism is also found in the epoch of kingship in the sphinx and in the depiction and naming of kings as "lions" and the like.

The earliest representations of large predators come from the cave paintings of the late Paleolithic period. A statuette of a man with a panther head is also known from this period.

In Native American sweat lodges, the large predator usually appears as the bear in the north, symbolizing strength and self-reliance.

The shaman was not the strongest in the field of hunting – but he was the stromgest in the field of the otherworld and therefore also in the field of magic. So he received the large predator as a mark too. In the Neolithic pictures and also still in the representations of the early Age of Kingdom the shamans can be recognized by the fact that they carry the fur of a large carnivore (panther, lion, tiger, leopard, puma, jaguar, bear etc.) or sometimes also sit on such a fur.

VI 3. The herd animal

Since herd animals appear in large numbers, they were the symbol of fertility and procreative power.

The earliest representations of herd animals come from the cave paintings of the late Paleolithic period. Also known from this time are rock engravings of dancing men with bull heads or deer antlers on their heads. These could be hunting spells, although it is more likely that the panther man is the hunter using magic – he identified with the large predator hunting successfully rather than the herd animal, i.e. the prey animal.

Therefore, the bull and deer dancers are more likely to refer to the idea that the (male) dead transform into a herd animal in the otherworld to preserve their procreative power so that they could successfully re-procreate themselves in the afterlife along with the afterlife mother goddess. The skin of the herd-animal, in wich the (male) dead was covered at his burial, was a kind of "magic viagra" for their re-procreation in the otherworld.

This is one of the most widespread mythological motifs, which has led to the many man/herd-animal hybrid figures: Pan, Fauns, Satyrs, Centaurs, Minotaur, etc. Much later they became the buck-legged and horned devil.

During the re-procreation the mother goddess took on the form of the corresponding female herd animal and became thus e.g. the cow-goddess Hathor, the goat goddess Heidrun, the mare goddess Epona, the sow goddess Nut and so on.

In the Indian sweat lodges, the herd animal appears as the White Buffalo Woman in the South, symbolizing fertility and community.

Since the shaman will also have accompanied the souls of the dead into the afterlife, he too appears in the guise of a herd-animal man – though this shaman figure is much rarer than the large carnivore man.

VI 4. The snake

The snake lives on the earth and dwells in caves and crevices, that is, in the earth. Since the dead are also buried in the earth, the dead were also depicted as snakes. Already at the beginning of the Neolithic Age, the way to the underworld was also seen as a snake.

From this derives, among other things, the motif of the giant snake: the path of the sun from its setting point in the west to its rising point in the east. When a general dry season began around 6000 B.C., this giant snake was interpreted as a rain robber, who was then defeated in autumn by the sky/sun god.

Through the connection of the ancestor-snake with the soul-bird and the burial-fire the winged, fire-spitting snake, i.e. the dragon, was created – later the horns of the herd-animals, the whiskers of a fish (soul in the water-underworld) and some other things were added, whereby the dragon became the general symbol of the ancestors and also of the afterlife-journeys.

The earliest depictions of snakes date back to the early Neolithic period, where they already appear as the spirit of the dead, the afterlife path, and the gifts of the dead. These gifts of the dead include the power and fire of the rising Kundalini serpent.

In the Indian sweat lodges, the serpent appears in the south and symbolizes the small, the hidden and the power of transformation.

For the shaman, the serpents are important as ancestral spirits, but the greatest significance is the awakening of the Kundalini serpent, which is closely related to astral travel and which also enables more effective magic.

VI 5. The Power Animal

Every human being has three "natural allies." When a soul incarnates, this soul has a certain character and certain intentions, which is shown, among other things, in the choice of the horoscope of its current incarnation.

This quality of the present incarnation of a soul is in resonance with the animal that has the dynamics most similar to the soul's character and intention: this is the power animal of the person concerned.

This quality of the present incarnation of a soul further resonates with the plant that has the attitude most similar to the essence and intention of the soul: that is the power plant of this person.

This quality of the present incarnation of a soul further resonates with the stone (mineral) that has the structure most similar to the essence and intention of the soul: that is the power stone of the subject.

These three connections, just like the horoscope, remain throughout life.

In the early cultures, these three allies, i.e. mainly the power animal, were recognized by omens at the birth of the subject or by conspicuous later events. Today one uses rather dream journeys for this purpose – alone or with the help of a shaman.

When a modern homeopath searches for a remedy for a patient, he also first asks himself whether the patient's problem is a structure (stone), an attitude (plant) or a movement (animal).

VI 6.   The Blood

Blood became a symbol of life very early. Already in the Old Stone Age 250,000 years ago, red ocher was used in rituals – presumably for body painting, which was supposed to increase the life force. This custom persisted into early royalty in Egypt.

VII   The Otherworld

The otherworld is the realm to which the shamans travel. The ideas about the other-world and the otherworld journey are therefore firmly connected with the shamans.

VII 1.   Otherworld and Souls

What is the Otherworld? The word in itself suggests a place that lies beyond the boundary between this world and the beyond – on the other side of the river at the boundary to the otherworld, on the other side of the bridge that spans this river, beyond the abyss, and so on. However, this "otherworld-place" is obviously to be understood only figuratively and not literally in the sense of a "2nd world", which lies under the surface of the earth, beyond the ocean of the world, somewhere in the stars etc., i.e. in a "place unreachable under normal circumstances".

What can be said for sure about the beyond is that the ancestors are there – not the bodies of the ancestors, which lie in their grave, but just the souls. The hereafter is therefore the realm of the souls.

It is obvious to ask whether the soul of a living person is in the same realm as the soul of a dead person. One could argue that the soul is nothing else than the level of consciousness, thus the "inside of the world". Then there would be no difference in principle between the soul of a living and a dead person – the soul of a living person would then only be bound to a body.

Therefore, it can be said that a shaman is essentially someone who is able to travel to the realm of souls or (to put more simply) who is able to contact souls – whether they are in a living or a dead person. The shaman would then be someone who can intentionally and fully consciously go to the "plane of the souls". The otherworld is probably nothing else than this "plane of the souls".

VII 2. The House of Consciousness

In order to better understand what the otherworld, the "plane of the souls", soul-consciousness, etc. actually are, it helps to take a closer look at consciousness itself.

The best known form of consciousness is the waking consciousness – which, for example, is reading these lines right now. It contains all the information that is necessary for the current situation: Perceptions, memories, intentions, thoughts, feelings, plans, etc.

The waking consciousness is like an office with a desk on which lies everything that is needed at the moment.

Then there is the subconsciousness – it is called "subconscious" because its contents are not in the waking consciousness. If all perceptions, all memories, all thoughts, all feelings would be conscious at the same time, the waking consciousness would be completely incapable of work – "input-overkill" …

Therefore the subconscious stays in the background and sends only those informations to the waking consciousness, that are needed at the moment – but e.g. when reading these lines not the memory of the date of the birthday of one's own maternal grandmother and also not the perception of one's own body weight on one's own butt, on which one is sitting at the moment.

The subconscious mind is like a big archive, from which you can bring all sorts of things into the office when you need them. As dreams, dream journeys, hypnoses, visions etc. show, this archive is not a chaotic accumulation of many memories, but a well sorted place.

The state of ecstasy is familiar to everyone, but only a few are familiar with it as a concept in everyday life. This state is characterized by the fact that the consciousness is completely focused on a single thing – it is "one-pointed". There are several forms of ecstasy: fear ecstasy, pain ecstasy, pleasure ecstasy, addiction ecstasy and meditative ecstasy, which is based on a deliberate and voluntary one-directed concentration.

In ecstasy, a single content fills the entire consciousness, causing particular states such as the panic attack, orgasm, or dharana (single-mindedness state) in meditation.

The ecstasy state is like the spotlight of a desk lamp on the office desk of the waking consciousness.

These three forms of consciousness are the possibilities of consciousness depending on the number of their contents – they are all three variants of perception, processing and direction of consciousness.

However, there is a fourth form of consciousness, which is of a slightly different nature than the three forms already described:

> Deep sleep consciousness is empty, it is silent, it is without content, it is "consciousness in itself." Thus it forms the basis of the other three forms of consciousness, which differ in the number of their contents: in the subconsciousness are all contents, in the waking consciousness are the contents needed at the moment, and in the ecstatic state is the one most important content.
>
> Thus, the deep-sleep consciousness can be thought of as the house containing the archive of the subconscious mind, the office of the waking conscious mind, and the spotlight of the ecstasy state.

Each of these four forms of consciousness has a specific brainwave frequency that can be measured with an EEG. Each consciousness is the "higher octave" of its underlying consciousness, i.e., it has a frequency twice as high.

The four forms of consciousness		
Consciousness	*Contents*	*EEG frequency*
Deep sleep consciousness	none	$\varnothing$ 3Hz (2-4Hz)
Subconsciousness	all	$\varnothing$ 6Hz (4-8Hz)
Waking consciousness	the important ones at the moment	$\varnothing$ 12Hz (8-16Hz)
Ecstasy	one	$\varnothing$ 24Hz (16-32Hz)

During meditation two or more of these states of consciousness are connected with each other, whereby the waking consciousness is present every time, because otherwise the state could not be evoked consciously and would not be experienced by the waking consciousness.

1. waking consciousness + deep sleep   = silence meditation (Zen)
2. waking consciousness + subconsciousness = dream journey
3. waking consciousness + ecstatic state   = tantra, kundalini, magic

The shamans use all three of these possibilities of "extraordinary states of consciousness":

1. With the silence meditation they reach the level of the souls.

2. With the dream journeys they receive telepathic information from the gods, the ancestors or in a direct way (e.g. finding lost things again). Through the dream journeys the shamans get in touch with the collective subconscious, which can be understood as a telepathically connected network of the subconscious of all now living and all deceased people. (The "city" in which the "house of consciousness" of a certain person stands.)

3. With the state of ecstasy, the shamans can completely focus on a single goal and thereby achieve a high telepathic/telekinetic intensity, which has a great magical effect.

The near-death experience, which is the basis of shamanism, contains all three elements:

1. The conscious encounter with one's own soul (corresponds to stillness meditation in terms of its effect),

2. the experience of going to the river at the border of the otherworld or similar, where one meets the souls of the deceased (corresponds to the dream journey), and

3. the high intensity, which is caused by being focused on the supposedly imminent own death (corresponds to ecstasy).

Thus the shamans are also "specialists of the three extraordinary states of consciousness" which are possible for humans.

VII 3. The otherworld-images of the shamans

Most elements of the otherworld-images of the religious epoch of Shamanism have already been described. Here follows again an overview:

- The soul is compared to a bird due to the "flying"-experience of astral projection during a near-death, and is therefore pictorially represented as a bird, i.e., a soul bird.
It later became the birds with human head, the humans with bird head, the humans with wings (angels), the humans with feathers, etc.

- Astral projection is closely associated with the experience of the rising Kundalini, because the experience of one of these experiences often leads to the experience of the other.

- The symbol of the near-death experience or the astral projection in general is the bird-stick: a stick on which a bird sits on top.
From it has evolved the totem pole, which is essentially a human being with his soul bird sitting on top. These totem poles then later became the staffs of the sweat lodge, menhirs, statues, the pillars in temples, the two pillars of the gateway to the otherworld, and so on. The world tree also shares this symbolism: a huge tree in whose crown the soul birds sit.

- The otherworld, i.e. the place where the dead are, was imagined as a "world under the earth's surface" due to the burial in the earth. Because of the fresh water bubbling up from the springs and the clouds (apparently) rising from the earth on the horizon, it was imagined that there was a huge fresh water lake under the earth, which was connected with the earth beyond to a water underworld.

- Because of the earth-underworld the ancestors could also be represented as snakes and because of the water-world also as fishes – but the fish-motif is quite rare compared to the soul-birds and the ancestor-snakes. There is also the motive of the souls as stars in the night-sky and also as blossoms in the crown of the world tree – these two motives probably originate only from the Neolithic Age.

- The arrival in the hereafter was conceived analogously to the arrival in the material world. In this way the three motives of the re-procreation, the re-birth and the re-breastfeeding came into being.

31

The procreation was connected with the procreative power and the fertility of the herd animals – so the motive of the procreation in the hereafter of the dead in the form of a bull, stallion, deer, boar, ram or he-goat with the mother goddess in the corresponding form of a cow, a mare, a hind, a sow, a sheep or a goat was created.

In this way the mixed forms of man and herd-animal arose: e.g. Zeus as a bull and Hathor as a cow; Poseidon as a stallion and Demeter as a mare; Cernunnos as a stag and the hind that suckled Sigurd-Siegfried; Freyr as a boar and Freya as a sow; sheep figures are quite rare; of the goat figures, Pan and the devil as a he-goat-man and Freya-Heidrun as a she-goat are known above all.

From the connection of the rebirth motif with the grain on the fields, the image of the god of grain, who is also the god of the dead has developed. The cyclic rebirth of the grain and thus also of the grain god every spring has contributed to the motif of reincarnation – which, of course, only says something about the placement of the reincarnation ideas in the overall mythological picture, but not about the reality of reincarnation itself.

Reincarnation has led to the symbol of the pregnancy-belly of the Mother Goddess, which is already known from the cave paintings of the late Paleolithic. Later it has evolved into the various ritual potions: the potion in the Hathor chalice among the Egyptians, the mead of the Celts and Germans, the nectar amrita of the Greeks, the soma of the Indians, the haoma of the Persians, the balché potion of the Mayans, the elixir of life of the alchemists in Europe and India, etc.

Since the Mother Goddess was the central figure in this world and in the hereafter, because without her the procreations, the births and the breast-feeding as well as the re-procreatioins, the re-births and the re-breastfeedings were impossible, she became a double goddess already in the late Paleolithic. She will have been the central reference person of the shamans until at least the middle Neolithic, before the sun god, became the father of the gods and eventually also the most important deity in the afterlife.

- An important place for the shamans has been the sweat lodge, because it has been the belly of the mother goddess and also the contact point to the ancestors. Graves have also been conceived as the womb of the mother goddess and thus associated with the sweat lodge. The later burial mounds were the belly of the pregnant earth goddess. Brushwood mounds, i.e. symbolic sweat lodges, were probably erected on graves already in the Paleolithic.

In the early Neolithic period, the sweat lodges became the half-stone sweat lodge temples of Göbekli Tepe, which then gradually developed into the classical temples, the pyramids and the stone circles.

During their otherworld journeys, the shamans sit either in the sweat lodge or on the tomb or mound of the dead person in question. From this the motif of the "shaman's seat" developed, which could be a brushwood layer, a pedestal, a flat table, a stool and the like.

- Fire may have been a symbol of warmth, life, and power as early as the Paleolithic – perhaps also of death and destruction.

VIII   Magic and Rituals

The shamans were responsible for various rituals – ultimately for all magical-religious activities.

VIII 1.   The otherworld journey

The most important ritual is undoubtedly the otherworld journey. There are essentially four variations of this:

1. the escorting of the dead to the otherworld at the time of burial;

2. the visit to the dead in the otherworld to receive advice and help from them;

3. the long-term bringing back of the dead to his skull, so that he is with his descendants during their lifetime, who still know him personally; and

4. the permanent retrieval of the dead man into his statue so that he will always protect the living.

VIII 2.   The firewalk

If one wanted to send something to the dead, one had to send it to the otherworld. However, only things that are dead can go to the otherworld (from a figurative logic point of view). For example, how can one kill a piece of meat or an apple? By cutting it up, destroying it in some other way, or by simply burning it. This is the origin of the very widespread burnt offerings from the Neolithic onwards – which are also known from the Old Testament, among others.

From this the (figurative) conclusion arose that also the dead could reach the hereafter most simply by burning. That is the origin of the cremation burial.

From these two symbolisms, in turn, it followed that the gateway to the afterlife must be a fire – after all, both the dead themselves and the offerings to them passed through the fire. This conception led e.g. with the Indo-Europeans to the fact that each ritual began with a fire or that in each temple an "eternal fire" must burn – after all the fire opens the gate to the beyond, in which the ancestors and the Gods are.

In this symbolism also lies the origin of incense – incense are burned parts of plants and resins … and in Egypt incense was called "senetjer", i.e. "that which makes divine", by which is meant that the incense calls the soul or deity into its statue. The incense, like the fire, opens the gate to the other world.

From this symbolism of the fire-otherworld gate it followed in turn that the shaman who wants to travel to the other world must go through a fire. This is how the firewalk, which is well known especially by the Indo-Europeans, came into being, in which one walks barefoot over a carpet of embers. However, such firewalks are also known from other peoples – in Hawaii the priests even walk barefoot over glowing lava.

The firewalk is a very real process without any trick – you can also strip naked and lie in the embers (I know this from my own experience).

From this complex fire symbolism many other motifs have arisen later, such as the fire spat by dragons (spirits of the dead), the flames glowing inside a tumulus (Germans), purgatory in hell (hell = cave = burial chamber of a tumulus), etc.

VIII 3.   The sweat lodge

The sweat lodge is connected with both the mother goddess and the ancestors: the lodge is the belly of the mother goddess and the staffs of the lodge are the ancestors who give support to their descendants.

Therefore, in the sweat lodge, people regain primordial trust, security, protection, support, strength, community and similar qualities.

VIII 4.   The summer procreation feast

Presumably, the midsummer procreation festival, which provided births at the beginning of spring, was also organized by the shamans. Probably they also asked the mother goddess for the fertility for the women and for the power of procreation for the men.

This festival later gave rise to the Holy Wedding of the King and the High Priest in Sumer, to the so-called "temple prostitution" in the whole Middle East, to the Tantra in India, to the diverse variants of the Walpurgis Night, which was strongly distorted by the Christian missionaries, to the summer sexual festival of the Dakota Indians, in which every man and woman is free to choose a partner, to some extent also to the Carnival, etc.

VIII 5. Hunting spells

The hunting spell has been associated with the transformation into the large predator, which has been the panther until the middle of the Neolithic period. Later lion, tiger, leopard, bear, jaguar etc. were added.

The mother goddess in the Old and New Stone Age was accompanied by two panthers, which shows that she was also a hunting goddess or at least gave her panther power to the hunters. Later her two panthers became two lions, leopards, cats, etc.

VIII 6. Fertility spells

The fertility spells have been associated with the herd animals – humans should become as procreative and fertile as the herd animals and reproduce in the same numbers.

Most probably, the fertility spells will have existed both in relation to this world, that is, in relation to living people, and in relation to the otherworld and the re-procreation of the deceased.

VIII 7. Healing

Healing by the shamans will probably have derived from their otherworld journeys: Since the shamans could bring back the whole soul of a fainting person into his body and could also bring the soul of the ancestors to their descendants to help them, it was natural to conceive of the illness as a "small death" and to regard the cause of the illness as the loss of a small part of the soul. In this way the worldwide spread shamanism motive of healing by bringing back a part of the soul came into being.

This form of healing can also be seen as re-integration of the psyche as well as trauma healing – quite an effective method.

Most likely, the shamanic healings will have been complemented by other healing methods such as wound dressings, dental treatments and herbal teas. Already for the

Old Stone Age amputations, operations and dental treatments like drillings and fillings are archaeologically proven – herbal teas are not directly provable, but extremely probable.

Possibly the shamans have quite early derived the willful and conscious dream journey to one's own soul from the unwilling near-death and the training of the repetition of this astal projection. This would then have been the greatest of all remedies for a diseased person.

VIII 8. Aids

There are some aids of the shamans that are widespread and well known. Among them are:

- the skins and masks of herd animals in fertility spells and the skins and masks of large predators in hunting spells, and, in general, probably the fox skin as a symbol of the otherworld journey;

- the frame drum (tambourine) and the dance as a method of ecstasy, where the drumhead of the drum was often painted with an otherworld map (usually the world tree);

- the sweat lodge, a tomb or altar with ancestor skulls as a ritual place;

- the symbolism:
  - red ocher   = blood, life force
  - bird   = soul
  - snake   = ancestor
  - fish   = ancestor
  - large predator   = strength
  - herd animal   = procreative power, fertility
    etc.

- the number symbolism:
  2 = this world and beyond, dual mother goddess.
  3 = plural, cycle, sun, rebirth
  4 = cardinal points, everywhere
  8 = great, complete, perfect

- Presumably, people experimented early on with various herbs that induced a death-like state, i.e. a near-death experience. The use of drugs in the cult is found in many nature-living peoples. Even in the mystery cults that emerged from the shamanic tradition around 600 BC, drugs may have been used to some extent.

However, the drugs are only an often dangerous aid to experiences that are also possible without drugs – after all, the aim is a near-death, which can also lead to a real death if the wrong dosage is used.

A similar approach is e.g. the method of the Celts to sink a druid aspirant, who was tied to a tree trunk, into a water-filled shaft and to pull him out and revive him only after he had almost drowned. That this method of coming to a near-death experience (astral projection) was life-threatening is obvious …

IX   The development of the shamans

The shamans are the magical-spiritual-religious specialists of the Paleolithic Age. When a new epoch arrived, they themselves also developed into something new.

The overview of this development helps to understand what shamans could be in the present time.

IX 1.   Paleolithic Age

Shamanism originated in the Paleolithic Age when some people attempted to repeat the astral projection during a near-death experience by willful decision and practice. This enabled them to contact the souls of the living and the souls of the dead.

In order to learn this, it will have been helpful even then to know a person who had already mastered it. Since in the small hunting communities of that time there will not always have been such a person, in such a case one often had to look for such a person in another clan. It is very likely that even after the end of the "shamanic education" there will have remained a contact between the two shamans and also with other shamans. In this way the first community was formed, which was not based on kinship ties, but on a common interest. This was the first association – it was still informal, but already non-profit …

The worldview of these shamans and of people in general at that time was based on associations. This is also the way the human subconsciousness is built up and this is also the way animals learn.

IX 2.   Neolithic Age

In the Neolithic the communities living together became much larger and therefore larger shamanic communities could emerge. They must have had a quite high form of organization, because they could coordinate up to 5000 people in the construction of the sweat lodge temples of that time e.g. in Göbekli Tepe (North Mesopotamia) around 10,000 BC. For these buildings, among other things, more than 5m high, complexly worked stone pillars and stone totem poles were made.

Among other things, they performed communal dances, which have been depicted, for example, around 7000 BC in Çatal Höyük.

The general world view at that time was based on analogies, i.e. parables. The use of analogies instead of associations had become necessary because there were too many people in a community to know each individual well enough. Hence, more abstract terms such as "hunter," "stonemason," "carpenter," "farmer," "sowing date," "potter's wheel axis," etc. emerged, all focusing on a single aspect of the people and things in question.

The most important analogy of the Neolithic period was the man/grain equation, which had come into being through agriculture, invented around 8500 BC. Sowing corresponds to procreation, germination to birth, growth to life, harvest to death, storage to dwelling in the otherworld, and re-sowing again to birth or rebirth.

The totality of these analogies, in which these "general concepts" were embedded, formed the mythology.

For each of these concepts and for each analogy there was a "right state" that was aimed at – the sowing date should be at the right time of the year, the axis of the potter's wheel should be straight, man should be in contact with his soul, etc. This correctness was represented by images and it was magically summoned – these are the statues, the temples and the rituals.

Thus, the shamans also became "keepers of the rightness". The most important symbol of this rightness was the security of the mother goddess, which was replaced by the cycle of the sun during the Neolithic period. When the wheel was invented, the perfect roundness of the wheel also became a symbol of correctness. The well-tuned strings of the lyre or harp also became a symbol too.

Since this correctness was represented and magically invoked by the shamans through rituals, the shamans also received the function of not only directly performing magically effective activities such as the otherworld journey or hunting spells, but also of performing symbolic rituals intended to represent and effect a general state. Thus, the shamans also became priests: the shaman does what is directly effective – the priest does what is indirectly, generally, and symbolically effective.

These shaman-priests also became the interpreters of oracles and dreams, and they were also responsible for discerning the future.

IX 3. Age of Kingship

In the epoch of kingship, which began around 3250 B.C. with the founding of the Egyptian kingdom, a centralization of the community organization to the king emerged.

Thus, the priest aspect was separated from the shaman-priests and developed into a priest hierarchy with the king at the top: the king guaranteed the rightness and the priests distributed it in the country.

However, the shaman aspect continued for a long time in the form of the funeral priests, the coronation priests, the otherworld journey priests, the healer priests and generally the magic priests. These shamans stood next to the general priestly hierarchy as a "priest with special duties" – he was turned to on special occasions, i.e. all kinds of crises: burials, coronations, healings, researching the future, and the like.

Around 600 B.C., from China to Western Europe, the initiation rituals of the Shaman, that had been developed as an "artificial near-death", were extended to the general public. In this way, the wisdom teachings, the meditation instructions and the mysteries came into being: Lao-tzu, Kungfu-tse, Tschung-tse, Buddha, Jaina, Patanjali, Zarathustra, Pythagoras, Zalmoxis, the Mysteries of Mithras, the Mysteries of Eleusis, the Mystries of Samothrace, the Mysteries of Sol Invictus, the initiation rituals of the Celts and the Teutons, etc.

Thus the shaman-priest also became the leader of the initiations, the priest of the mysteries, the sage of the knwledge of the otherworld, and the teacher of meditation. The principle of the Mysteries could be paraphrased as "Everybody a shaman!" and "Each one is his own king!". The central element of the Mysteries (that was written on the doors of the oracle of Delphi) was naturally the "Nothing in excess!" which leads to the "Know thyself!" … the encounter with one's own soul.

The archetype of this striving and these shaman initiation priests is Odin with the Teutons, Cernunnos with the Celts, Mithras with the Persians, Krishna with the Indians, Christ with the Jews and so on.

The worldview that emerged anew in this epoch is philosophy: everything is derived from a first cause and explained with it as well as from it – as a rule, God is this first cause. Philosophy is the centralization in thought. The application of this centralization to the inner attitude is meditative concentration; the aid of this single-mindedness is the mystery rituals; and the goal of this centralization in each individual is the recognition and experience of one's own soul, which in turn leads to self-responsible action … "Each one is his own king!"

IX 4. Age of Materialism

In materialism, man, who has become independent in the previous epoch, regards the world as an object in front of him. Because man has become "his own king", he can take a distance to the world and examine the individual things in the world objectively. Thereby the materialism with its discoveries, inventions and explorations as well as with the industrialization resulting from it as practical application originated from approx. 1500 A.D..

The people, who would have become shamans in the earlier epochs, became now researchers, inventors and discoverers. First of all, from this new group of people there was no more connection with the earlier shamans except for the curious and inquisitive attitude of mind.

Only in Spiritism, which preserved the ancestor cult of the shamans from the Old and New Stone Age, as well as in the priests, who had become mystics, the old spiritual-magical urge for knowledge lived on. Only when the first researchers turned to the human psyche and founded psychology, something like "scientific shamans" emerged: the psychologists and therapists.

IX 5. Age of Globalization

After the two world wars, a new attitude of mind arose from the realization that the focus on the individual and the short-sighted egoism of the nation-states and the free market economy were not sufficient to prevent a general destruction of human beings by themselves.

This led to many new developments

- the foundation of the UN and its subdivisions such as the WHO,
- the nuclear disarmament,
- the realization of the limits of growth,
- the attempts to limit overpopulation,
- the emergence of ecology,
- the development of new models of relationships,
- the boom of psychology,
- the re-integration of the ancient shamanic method of "ancestor worship" in the form of systemic family constellations,
- the renaissance of ancient religions,
- the efforts to create a cooperation of all religions and a synthesis of all religions,
- the penetration especially of physics and astronomy into areas which are far beyond the usual conceptions and show many similarities with the former magical-mythological-religious world views,
- the increasing re-intagration of the scientific worldview of materialism with the magical worldview of the Paleolithic, the Neolithic and the epoch of kingship,
etc.

From these development approaches in the new "globally oriented" world view, which begins to develop since approx. 1950, can be derived, what a shaman could be nowadays.

This will be considered in more detail in the next chapter.

X   Shamans today

In a book about shamanism, the question of what a shaman can or should be today, and why it might still be desirable for shamans to exist at all, is the central point …

If there should be no conclusive answer to this question, shamanism would be only an old form of religion from former times and at most from an academic point of view of moderate interest.

If there should be no answer to this question, basically also this book would be more or less superfluous – then I would not have written it either …

X 1.   The reasonable use of the term "shaman"

It is not possible to decide who should be called a "shaman" and who should not – in the end it simply results from the collective use of this term … the most common definition will prevail.

Generally speaking, one can say for all terms that too narrow a definition of a term usually results in a term being sharply defined but rarely used. Of course, this does not apply to unambiguous basic terms such as "iron", "walk" or "red".

If you define a term too broadly, its outline becomes fuzzy. Then it is used a lot, but does not say too much for sure anymore.

Finally, it can be observed that a term is most alive when it has a great meaning for the general public – but this does not depend on the definition of the term, but on that, what is signified by this term.

If you use "shaman" in the very classical way as "person with a near-death experience who has used this experience to make contact with souls", you are on the safe side. Nevertheless, one will not necessarily have to think of a hunting accident with the near-death experience as in former times in the Old Stone Age, but perhaps rather of a traffic accident, an awakening from a chloroform anesthesia, while one still floats (in the astral body) over his body, or similar.

Also the contact to the ancestors will probably be considered rather in a modern way like e.g. in spiritism or in family constellations – even if the ancestor invocations in sweat lodge ceremonies can certainly also occur.

Well, in the end this consideration is actually idle, because although one can decide for oneself how one wants to use the term "shaman", one has only a very small influence on how it will be used in general.

X 2. Shamanism and Globalization

In today's era of globalization, which began around 1950, many shamanic activities have taken on a new form. If we look at the classical activities of shamans and their present forms, we already get a fairly well contoured picture of what a shaman might be today.

- The shaman is essentially someone who knows his own soul (astral body) and therefore secondarily is also able to recognize the soul of other people or can help others to recognize their own soul.

In shamanism, a near-death experience usually leads to this experience. However, other methods are also conceivable: the sun dances from the Neolithic Age, the mysteries and meditations from the epoch of kingship and the psychological methods from the age of materialism.

- Then a shaman is also a researcher – otherwise he would not have developed his near-death experience into his shaman position.

Thus, a shaman in today's time would also be a researcher who wants to understand the world and is looking for a comprehensive world view that includes magic, religion and spirituality as well as the natural sciences.

- Then a shaman is also someone who helps people in his community – the shaman-priest of the ancient Egyptians, who undertook the otherworld journey to the dead during burials, was called "sem", i.e. simply "helper".

So a person who could be called a "shaman" in modern times should also have the wish to help others: a doctor, a healer, a nurse, a therapist, a social worker, a yoga teacher, a sweat lodge leader, a firewalking leader, a magic teacher, etc.

- A shaman, at least in Neolithic times, also has the task of leading the rituals that (re)establish rightness.

Therefore, leading rituals and also other social-organizational tasks would be something that traditionally belongs to a shaman: the leader of an order of magicians, the leader of a witch coven, a priest in a church, the leader of a Caritas institution, the organizator of a mystery school, the founder of an astrology school and much more.

- A shaman is also able to receive messages from the gods and the ancestors.

A modern shaman should therefore also have this ability: through the well-practiced use of tarot cards, as an astrologer, as a leader of family constellations, through dream journeys, through spiritualistic sessions and such methods more.

- A shaman is in some respects also a carrier and preserver and developer of the magical-religious-spiritual aspect of his culture.

Therefore, a modern shaman should also have a worldview that is based on solid experiences and is coherent in itself. It would also be very pleasant if he knows his own style and therefore also the limits and emphases of his own worldview – this would give him some tolerance towards other world-views. He could be a historian of religion, a philosopher, a practitioner of magic, and all sorts of other things – or all of these at once, which would be best, of course.

- One task of the shaman is also to care for the well-being of his community.

This would not only include psychological and social knowledge – also an ecological engagement and activities in the peace movement would be very suitable and furthermore all similar activities, which serve the preservation of the possibility of people to continue to live on this earth.

- Finally, shamans are also magic-knowledgeable.

So a modern shaman should be able to use telepathy, deal with homeopathy, make effective talismans, recognize power animals, perform firewalks, perform hypnosis, teach combat magic, etc.

The demands on a modern shaman are not exactly low – but they won't have been in the late Paleolithic either …

X 3. Shaman Syncretism

There are many shamanic traditions – those of the many different Indian tribes, those of the Siberian peoples, those of the African tribes, those of the Australian Aborigines, those of the inhabitants of Oceania, the half-forgotten traditions of the Teutons, Celts, Persians and other Indo-European peoples, then also the tradition of the mysteries and meditation teachings founded around 600 B.C., and also some psychological directions – especially those of C.G. Jung.

There is no "right" and no "wrong" tradition or lore, and also no "appropriate", "inappropriate", "contemporary", "untimely" etc. direction, because all shamanic traditions are based on the same foundation.

- The shamans invoke different deities – but they all know the Mother Goddess.

- The shamans used different methods – but they all have the same goal.

- The shamans have different focuses in their activities – but the center is always the souls of the people.

It follows that in today's globalized times, when all these different traditions are to some extent available to everyone, a syncretic approach is the most sensible way to proceed: everyone looks for the teacher, the method and the focus that best suits him.

This results in mixed methods that blithely combine African sun dances, the Jungian concept of the collective unconsciousness, ancient Egyptian deities, Dervish dances, Hawaiian firewalks, Native American sweat lodges, South American ayahuasca ceremonies, South African family constellations, European spiritism, the rituals of the Golden Dawn, and much more.

From this colorful mixture, the foundations common to all systems will then gradually emerge and one will recognize more and more clearly the basic principles underlying all these methods. In this way, the "neo-shamans" will also participate in the new world view of the globalization epoch, which has been gradually emerging since 1950.

- The world view of the Old Stone Age corresponds to the baby: a life as a part of nature in nature or as a baby in symbiosis with the mother – Freund's "oral phase" … a "Yes".

- The world view of the Neolithic era corresponds to the infant: the molding of parts of nature into the culture of agriculture and animal husbandry and villages, respectively, an imprinting of one's environment through walking, acting and speech – Freud's "anal phase" … a "No!"

- The world view of the epoch of royalty corresponds to the child: the centralization of the whole culture on the king, the truth and God resp. the centering of the psyche on the ego and finally on the soul – Freud's "phallic phase" … an "I!!!"

- The world view of materialism corresponds to the pubescent: exploring and using the whole world or testing one's own power and searching for a suitable relationship – Freud's "genital phase" … a "You?"

- The world view of globalization corresponds to the adult: the search for a stable system of humanity on earth or for a stable system of the family through the parents – the "adult phase" … a "We."

In the first phase of evolution the "Yes" of the baby and the "No!" of infant merge into the "I!!!" of the child.

In the second phase of evolution the "I!!!" of the child and the "You?" of the youth merge into the "We." of the adult.

The third phase of evolution lies still in the future – then the "We." of the adult and the "Other …" of the older man merge into the "All" of the old man.

So, the shamans currently have the rather daunting task of helping to develop a world design that gives everyone a chance to live and preserves the Earth as our foundation for life. It would be helpful if the shamans became role models for "being parents" … "parents of their children" and "parents of the earth".

This is only possible in a system in which the demarcations are dissolved and in which the individuality is no longer protected by demarcation but by self-certainty. For this a far-sighted egoism is needed, which overlooks the next 10 to 20 conse-quences. The struggle between the old, partly narcissistic, short-sighted egoism and the new, far-sighted egoism can be observed in all corners of current politics.

The two important aspects of a world view without boundaries are responsibility and trust: to bear the whole in responsibility and to be borne by the whole in trust.

Finally, there is one more aspect of this new world view: it can only work if the majority of people acquire the necessary insights, the necessary far-sightedness and therefore the far-sighted egoism. This means that this new world order cannot be invented or decreed, but that it must arise in (almost) all people – it is a "grassroots revolution".

For shamans this means that ultimately everyone has to become a shaman, at least to some extent.

With this, the term "shaman" has of course now been extended very far, but it is still sufficiently sharply contoured to contain a clear statement.

X 4.   How can one become a shaman today?

In the Rhineland they say "every Jeck is different" ... A "Jeck" ist a masqueraded participant of carnival.

This wise saying is also true for the way to become a shaman: there is no uniform way. One can enumerate possible elements of this path, whereby they have all already been mentioned in this book. It is also not enough to have a single one of these approaches, but it must be a larger group of these approaches that lead to the fact that one can reasonably call oneself a "shaman".

- Near-death experiences
- Meditation experiences with one's own soul
- Dream journeys
- Family Constellations
- Mystery initiations
- Sweat lodges
- Firewalks
- Invocations of the dead ("necromancy")
- Rituals
- Psychology
- Therapy
- Astrology
- Interpretation of omens and oracles
- Peace activities
- Non-violent communication
- Being present in the here and now
- Ecological engagement
- Cooperation in nuclear, biological and chemical disarmament
  etc.

- - -

The important thing is not to become a shaman or to be called a "shaman" by others, but to recognize and do what one wants, and also to recognize and do what is necessary for the survival of our species on earth. If this becomes the essential characteristic of a shaman today, then it is good to be a shaman.

English Books by Harry Eilenstein

- Living Magic (261 p.)
- The Synthesis of Physics and Magic (192 p.)
- Astral Projection for Beginners (60 p.)
- Invocations for Beginners (52 p.)
- Evocations for Beginners (62 p.)
- Auto-Movement for Beginners (60 p.)
- Elves for Beginners (56 p.)
- Hypnosis for Beginners (56 p.)
- Shamanism for Beginners (52 p.)
  These books will be puplished soon:
- Telepathy for Beginners
- Telepathy for Advanced Learners
- Telekinesis for Beginners
- Life Force for Beginners
- Meditation for Beginners
- Kundalini for Beginners
- Chakra-Magic for Beginners
- Astrology for Beginners
- Ritual Magic for Beginners
- Mandalas for Beginners
- Money Magic for Beginners
- Love Magic for Beginners
- Magic Research for Beginners
- Self-awareness for Beginners
- Symbolism of Numbers for Beginners
- Language of the Moon – for Beginners
- Magic Chant for Beginners
- Prophecy for Beginners
- Magic Objects for Beginners
- Da'ath-Magic for Beginners
- Crop Circles for Beginners
- Feng Shui for Beginners
- Magic for Beginners – Anthology I
- Magic for Beginners – Anthology II
- Magic for Beginners – Anthology III
- Magic for Beginners – Anthology IV

Bücher von Harry Eilenstein

Religion allgemein
- Die sieben Schritte des Lebens (428 S.)
- Muttergöttin und Schamanen (168 S.)
- Göbekli Tepe (472 S.)
- Die Göttin von Göbekli Tepe (144 S.)
- Totempfähle (440 S.)
- Christus (60 S.)
- Dakini (80 S.)
- Vajra (76 S.)

Ägypten
- Hathor und Re 1: Götter und Mythen im Alten Ägypten (432 S.)
- Hathor und Re 2: Die altägyptische Religion – Ursprünge, Kult und Magie (396 S.)
- Isis (508 S.)

Indogermanen
- Die Entwicklung der indogermanischen Religionen (700 S.)
- Wurzeln und Zweige der indogermanischen Religion (224 S.)

Germanen
- Die Götter der Germanen (87 Bände – siehe nächste Seite)
- Odin (300 S.)

Kelten
- Cernunnos (690 S.)
- Taliesin (228 S.)
- Der Kessel von Gundestrup (220 S.)
- Der Chiemsee-Kessel (76)

Psychologie
- Über die Freude (100 S.)
- Das Geheimnis des inneren Friedens (252 S.)
- Das Beziehungsmandala (52 S.)
- Gefühle und ihre Verwandlungen (404 S.)
- einsgerichtet (140 S.)
- Liebe und Eigenständigkeit (216 S.)
- Von innerer Fülle zu äußerem Gedeihen (52 S.)

Heilung
- Die Symbolik der Krankheiten (76 S.)

Kunst
- Herz des Tanzes – Tanz des Herzens (160 S.)

Drama
- König Athelstan (104 S.)

Bücher von Harry Eilenstein

„Magie für Anfänger"

- Telepathie für Anfänger (60 S.)
- Telepathie für Fortgeschrittene (52 S.)
- Telekinese für Anfänger (52 S.)
- Lebenskraft für Anfänger (60 S.)
- Meditation für Anfänger (56 S.)
- Kundalini für Anfänger (100 S.)
- Hypnose für Anfänger (56 S.)
- Auto-Movement für Anfänger (56 S.)
- Chakra-Magie für Anfänger (148 S.)
- Astralreisen für Anfänger (56 S.)
- Astrologie für Anfänger (120 S.)
- Ritual-Magie für Anfänger (56 S.)
- Mandalas für Anfänger (68 S.)
- Geldzauber für Anfänger (56 S.)
- Liebeszauber für Anfänger (52 S.)
- Invokationen für Anfänger (52 S.)
- Evokationen für Anfänger (60 S.)
- Elfen für Anfänger (56 S.)
- Magie-Forschung für Anfänger (140 S.)
- Selbsterkenntnis für Anfänger (52 S.)
- Zahlensymbolik für Anfänger (60 S.)
- Die Sprache des Mondes – für Anfänger (116 S.)
- Zaubergesänge für Anfänger (100 S.)
- Zukunftschau für Anfänger (60 S.)
- Schamanismus für Anfänger (52 S.)
- Magische Gegenstände für Anfänger (68 S.)
- Da'ath-Magie für Anfänger (64 S.)
- Kornkreise für Anfänger (348 S.)
- Feng Shui für Anfänger (96 S.)
- Magie für Anfänger – Sammelband I (696 S.)
- Magie für Anfänger – Sammelband II (664 S.)
- Magie für Anfänger – Sammelband III (580 S.)

„Traumreisen"

- Traumreisen zu Heilpflanzen (700 S.)

Magie

- Handbuch für Zauberlehrlinge (408 S.)
- Tarot (104 S.)
- Physik und Magie (184 S.)
- Die Synthese von Physik und Magie (200S.)
- Die Magie-Formel (156 S.)
- Krafttiere – Tiergöttinnen – Tiertänze (112 S.)
- Schwitzhütten (524 S.)
- Mythen und Magie der Harfe (116 S.)
- Magie heute – Berichte aus der Praxis (288 S.)

Meditation

- Der Lebenskraftkörper (230 S.)
- Die Chakren (100 S.)
- Das Chakren-System mit den Nebenchakren (296 S.)
- Organe und Chakren (64 S.)
- Die platonischen Körper in den Chakren (156 S.)
- Meditation (140 S.)
- Drachenfeuer (124 S.)
- Kundalini I (676 S.)
- Reinkarnation (156 S.)
- einsgerichtet (140 S.)

Astrologie

- Astrologie (496 S.)
- Photo-Astrologie (428 S.)
- Die astrologischen Aspekte (88 S.)
- Horoskop und Seele (120 S.)

Kabbala

- Kursus der praktischen Kabbala (150 S.)
- Eltern der Erde (450 S.)
- Blüten des Lebensbaumes:
    - Die Struktur des kabbalistischen Lebensbaumes (370 S.)
    - Der kabbalistische Lebensbaum als Forschungshilfsmittel (580 S.)
    - Der kabbalistische Lebensbaum als spirituelle Landkarte (520 S.)

Die Themen der 87 Bände der Reihe „Die Götter der Germanen"